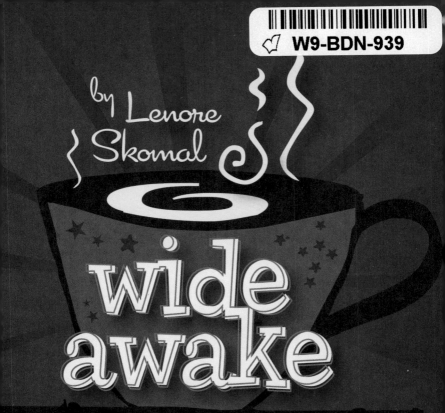

by Lenore Skomal

wide awake

the INSOMNIAC'S MANIFESTO to RULING THE WORLD

CIDER MILL PRESS

BOOK PUBLISHERS

kennebunkport, maine

13 Digit ISBN: 978-1-60433-005-2
10 Digit ISBN: 1-60433-005-8

This book may be ordered by mail from the publisher. Please include $2.00 for postage and handling. Please support your local bookseller first!

Books published by Cider Mill Press Book Publishers are available at special discounts for bulk purchases in the United States by corporations, institutions, and other organizations. For more information, please contact the publisher.

Cider Mill Press Book Publishers
"Where good books are ready for press"
12 Port Farm Road
Kennebunkport, Maine 04046

Visit us on the web!
www.cidermillpress.com

Design by Jessica Disbrow Talley

Printed in China

1 2 3 4 5 6 7 8 9 0
First Edition

This book is dedicated to
all the insomniacs and
night owls of the universe.
Rise up, brethren,
and take your rightful
place at the top of the
pecking order.

Table of Contents

Introduction

Insomnia:
Curse or Blessing?

You've heard the hype—you need to sleep. At least eight hours a night. And if you don't, well, the consequences are grave, ranging from lack of concentration to a virtual collapse of all your bodily functions. If you listen to the naysayers, chronic lack of sleep will leave you a blithering, bleary lump of quivering flesh, barely inches away from your grave.

Says who? The experts, of course. And as history has shown us time and again, you know how much they can be trusted. Here is the definitive dope, right here in this book, that will rattle your beliefs about sleep, challenge the establishment's current view of just how much sleep you need, and hopefully offer you a healthier way of looking at yourself and your sleep patterns. And at the very least, wake you up to the fact that you can count yourself as one of a much greater whole—the wakeful masses.

If you are a chronic insomniac, and it is assumed you are if you picked up this book, not only do you have to contend with your inability to sleep—which has been labeled a "disorder"—you also have to swallow a heaping helping of shame to go along with it, as well as quell the furtive need to justify your way of life.

They say that we sleep one-third of our lives away. Doesn't that sound like a colossal waste? Did you ever once take this issue of insomnia out of the box that society has crammed it in, turn it around, and look at it from other perspectives? You might just realize that maybe there isn't something wrong with you at all. Perhaps you are part of a superior breed, fine-tuned to be able to exist, function, and even excel on minimal sleep. Like a hybrid engine, you may just burn more efficiently. Maybe you are destined to do great things, while others of a meeker nature have their eyes closed.

But this requires a shift in your paradigm, a general debunking of the myths about sleep in general, a hard look at supposed cure-alls for insomnia, and some ideas about what you could be doing, next to ruling the world, if you actually were productive during your insomniac hours.

Simply put: if you were to fully accept your insomnia as a blessing, imagine what great things you could do!

(Note: This book was written, researched, edited, and produced by insomniacs, all working between the hours of 1:00 and 5:00 a.m., EST. No fully rested human was consulted in its production or even allowed to touch it for that matter.)

SLEEP MYTHS

Concern or Conspiracy?

• CHAPTER 1 •

All the so-called sleep experts

spend their waking hours—of which they have very few, by the way—compiling lists of ways to get the rest of us to fall asleep and stay there. Of course, this begs the question of why. What exactly is their motive?

To this end, their efforts are spent sitting around all day and night doing sleep studies and conducting the all-important sleep-related research, much of it funded by the federal government and powerful pharmaceutical companies. This data gives additional fodder to those industries dependent on getting humanity to fall asleep and stay that way for at least seven to nine hours a night. Sounds a bit worrisome, doesn't it?

You Have a Problem

Like most of the people on this planet (or at least the Western hemisphere), if you do not fall into the sleep patterns that have been established as normal and average for the rest of the human race, you have undoubtedly been led to believe that you have a problem—that you have a sleeping disorder. You most likely have been labeled a night owl, insomniac, and sleep-deprived. Talking about your insomnia has solicited one of several patterned responses: sympathy—"Oh you poor thing"; helpfulness—"Have you tried soaking in formaldehyde?"; anger—"What the hell is wrong with you!"; and judgment—"No wonder you're so cranky." This may have led you to feel like a freak. It is highly doubtful that anyone has clapped you on the back and said, "I am so jealous! What did you accomplish between the hours of 2:30 and 5:00 this morning?" Nope, you'll never hear it.

Insomnia is looked at as a bad thing, a pitiable thing, something to be worried about, like early onset hair loss, ugly babies, and losing the lottery. The truth is, insomnia might just be a good thing.

Do you know anyone, who isn't a teenager that is, who can actually sleep the requisite seven to nine hours? Someone who falls easily into a deep, peaceful slumber and snoozes right through the night without interruption?

Probably not. And if you do, those folks are the exception, not the rule. Has this not struck you as strange, especially when we are continually reminded that we all should be doing it? If most adults cannot adhere or ascribe to what we are told is the holistically healthy norm of sleep at night, then who is it that is getting all that sleep? Are these medical experts basing this baseless information on nomadic tribes from New Zealand? Or is it merely another old wives' tale that has been passed on from generation to generation, like your Nonna's lasagna recipe?

The New Normal

We may never truly know, unless we take a massive head count, if insomniacs are really the majority—the new "normal," so to speak. But the stigma abounds that insomniacs are not—we are a slim slice of the population that needs pills, ambient noise, aromatherapy, and lots of bamboo stalks sprinkled in the eastern corners of our homes. We need help. The motivation in having us believe we are infirmed and paltry in population keeps us down on the farm—manageable, divided, and more than an arm's grasp away from discovering that there is strength in numbers. Face it, knowing you can't sleep, especially in the dark wee hours of the morning, can be an overwhelming and helpless feeling. You feel all alone—especially when you are the only one in your house counting backwards from 10,000 and counting how many times the radiator bangs. You are vulnerable, and those who are out to get you know it.

This could be part of a bigger conspiracy, one that might also involve the strange disappearance of Amelia Earhart, JFK's assassination, the establishment of a New World Order. Ever hear of the Trilateral Commission? Perhaps the propaganda that is out there—glibly disguised as attempts to aid us, the pathetic and over-tired—is really a feeble attempt by the sleep-enriched to quell the competition—us—and ultimately take over the world, in a Donald Trumpian way, and perhaps the universe.

More likely than not, they're also jealous. Because of their weaker constitutions, these poor souls live to fall into bed at the end of the day. They literally love sleep. Their minds can't function after being awake a mere twelve hours, so they often clock out of work at 5:00 and are asleep by the time the sun goes down—or wish they were. Face it: these sleep-saturated souls are not the sleep experts. If you really look at the issue, we are the sleep experts. There isn't an insomniac awake who doesn't know the A to Z of sleeping disorders.

Stick with the truth. It's a known fact that insomniacs of the world have fueled a multi-billion-dollar sleep aids industry—which is essentially drugging us and rendering us useless to fight back. The method in their madness is to slowly undermine our self-confidence by purporting the age-old myth that humans need sleep to survive and thrive. They then line up expert after so-called expert to underscore this, padding their opinion with myopic research and unsubstantiated studies. This has established the baseline hypothesis that we all need to sleep the same set number of hours each night. As a society, once we bought into that, it would only make sense to assume that those who have trouble getting sleep or staying asleep—like us—must have something wrong with them. Logically, the next step is to fix us.

Why Fix What Isn't Broken?

It's genius, really. And that premise alone—that we are disabled—has turned us into a huge, highly attractive market that now feeds upon itself. To come out with the truth would mean to conduct studies that have never been done. Studies that would prove that sleep is an individual need, patterned and conditioned from not only genetics, but lifestyle, physiology, psychology, and how much you idolize Paris Hilton.

It's no wonder (and hardly surprising) that there is very little data or scientific study on whether insomnia could actually be a good thing. You know, something that looks at insomnia not just as a condition that runs a body ragged and into a state of dire breakdown and collapse. Those studies are as common as dew in Dixie. Try to find more than one study that looks at whether insomnia might actually feed the creative soul, fuel the spiritual muse, and herald unbounding creativity.

There is one study that suggests that insomnia and originality might go hand-in-hand. In keeping with the study's iconoclastic thrust, the title presents the hypothesis as a question: "Could Creativity Be Associated With Insomnia?" Authors Dione Healey of the University of Canterbury and Mark A. Runco of California State University at Fullerton, worked with sixty New Zealand children between the ages of ten and twelve, half of whom scored in the 90th percentile or better on a standard creativity test, while the other half fell short of that mark. Healey and Runco found that seventeen of the thirty highly creative children showed signs of sleep disturbance, and they reported their findings in the *Creativity Research Journal*–hardly the *New England Journal of Medicine*. Still, over half the kids who suffered from insomnia scored in the highest percentile.

Of course, the authors cited that this study left many open-ended questions and deferred from coming out and actually saying that there were any positive aspects to those who lacked sleep.

So much of the data we have left is what has been fed to us as shut-eye pablum over the ages and is, quite frankly, nothing more than classic snake oil salesmanship and cheap huckstering. Some of the myths need to be dealt with directly.

Myth:

Everyone needs at least seven hours of sleep a night.

Reality:

This is ridiculous. When it comes to needs, face it, the list is limited: food and water, shelter, and reality TV. There is a remote pygmy tribe in central Australia that never sleeps. Their tribal grand marshal is 186 years old. In dog years. Saying that each unique individual has the same exact needs as the next unique individual is not only stupid, it's presumptuous, stereotypical, possibly racist, maybe egocentric, and definitely not politically correct. It's like telling us we all need to eat sixteen hot dogs a week. Or like saying that everybody's body temperature is 98.6° F. Come on.

Myth:

Over time, chronic lack of sleep wears down your body.

Reality:

Poppycock. Anyone who doesn't sleep on a regular basis can contend beyond a shadow of a doubt that lack of sleep actually improves eyesight, sharpens all the senses, creates much more laughter in our lives (delirium will do that), and is the best emotional therapy in the world, because most insomniacs are more in tune with their raw emotions. Hence, they cry, scream, quicken to temper, and react much more hastily than solid sleepers, getting to the point faster and trimming their lives down to the barest of necessities—and getting rid of thin-skinned friends for that matter, too. Chronic lack of sleep is also the best cure-all for insomnia—the one surefire way to ensure a good sleep.

Myth:

Well-rested people wake up happier,
more energetic, and ready to face the day.

Reality:

Yeah, right! That is, until they faint face down in their cold chicken casseroles at 8:00 p.m. because they are on the slippery slope of addiction and can't keep their eyes open. They are, quite frankly, exhausted. The dark truth is: sleep is highly addictive. The more you get, the more you want. Studies have shown that by the time these seven-to-nine-hour-a-nighters are seventy, they are sleeping an average of 150 hours a week. It's true.

There are songs, movies, books, poetry and even a video game about insomnia (*Crush*). Of the nineteen songs written, nine of them are entitled "Insomnia." The others include such catchy titles as "Melatonin," "Brainstew," and "Who Needs Sleep?"

Movies in Pop Culture:

Cashback (2006)
The Machinist (2004)
Lost In Translation (2003)
Insomnia (2002)
Fight Club (1999)
Insomnia (1997)
Dream of an Insomniac (1996)
Prelude to a Kiss (1992)
The Cure for Insomnia (1987)
Taxi Driver (1976)

Books:

Insomnia, Stephen King
Fight Club, Chuck Palahniuk
Johnny the Homicidal Maniac, Jhonen Vasquez

You're
in
Good &
Company

FAMOUS
INSOMNIACS

◖ CHAPTER 2 ◗

You are in good company.

If more proof is needed that sleep is a myth purported by the fearful and sleep-enriched, then all you have to look at is the list of famous insomniacs who did amazing things to change, entertain, and comment on the world. Some say our national sleep debt began when Thomas Edison, who slept only four hours a day, believed that too much shut-eye was unhealthy and made people stupid. There you have it. Other insomniacs include Catherine the Great, Charles Dickens, Cary Grant, Marcel Proust, and the following:

Alexandre Dumas

after trying many remedies was advised by a famous doctor to get out of bed when he couldn't sleep. He became addicted to late-night strolls.

Franz Kafka

was a miserable insomniac and kept a diary detailing his suffering. For October 2, 1911, he wrote, "Sleepless night. The third in a row. I fall asleep soundly, but after an hour I wake up, as though I had laid my head in the wrong hole."

Mark Twain

chronic non-sleeper was once at a friend's house. His bedroom was poorly ventilated and he could not sleep. Convinced it was the lack of fresh air, he picked up his shoe and threw it through the darkness at the window, which he had been unable to open. He heard the sound of breaking glass, rolled over, and fell fast asleep. The light of the next morning revealed that the glass he had broken belonged to a bookcase in the room. The window was still closed.

Theodore Roosevelt

found his insomnia cure was a shot of cognac in a glass of milk.

Winston Churchill

took catnaps to help him get through his sleepless nights.

Ben Franklin

was a fresh air fanatic. He once had to share a room with a man who could not sleep with the window open. Franklin won the ensuing debate, and the shutters were opened wide and he slept soundly. His roommate did not sleep a wink. In the morning, however, they discovered that the shutters they had opened to let in the fresh air actually opened onto a small closet.

Marlene Dietrich

swore the only way she could lull herself to sleep was with a sardine and onion sandwich.

Amy Lowell

the poet reserved five rooms when she stayed in a hotel—one to sleep in, and empty rooms above, below, and on either side, in order to guarantee quiet.

Tallulah Bankhead

suffered from severe insomnia. She hired young homosexual "caddies" to keep her company, and one of their most important duties was to hold her hand until she drifted off to sleep.

W. C. Fields

resorted to rather unusual methods of his own to usher in sleep. A big fan of haircuts, he would stretch out in a barber's chair with towels wrapped around him until he felt drowsy. When the chair didn't do the trick, he tried stretching out on his pool table or falling asleep under a beach umbrella being sprinkled by a garden hose. His explanation: "Somehow a moratorium is declared on all my troubles when it is raining."

Marilyn Monroe

the troubled film star was a regular insomniac and frequently took sleeping pills in order to get to sleep. Over the years, her insomnia grew steadily worse until her death, supposedly from an overdose of sleeping tablets.

Vincent Van Gogh

preferred to treat his insomnia himself. The artist's remedy involved a strong dose of camphor applied to his mattress and pillow. This may have helped him sleep, but it also steadily poisoned him.

Napoleon Bonaparte

built an empire on a few hours of sleep at a time. The "Little Emperor" suffered so frequently from insomnia, rarely sleeping more than four hours a night, that he simply learned to live with the condition.

Judy Garland

as a teenager was prescribed amphetamines to control her weight. As the years went by, she took so many that she sometimes stayed up three or four days running. She added sleeping pills to her regimen, and her insomnia and addiction increased. She eventually died of a drug overdose.

Margaret Thatcher

the redoubtable British prime minister was famous for only needing four or fewer hours of sleep a night. Her motto: "Sleep is for wimps."

Groucho Marx

whose insomnia started following the stock market crash of 1929 in which he lost a small fortune—namely, $240,000 in forty-eight hours. To ease the symptoms of insomnia, Groucho would call strangers up in the dead of night and insult them.

Famous Sleepers:
Look where it got them!

If sleeping is so good for you, why is it that the world's two most famous sleepers never really accomplished much in their lifetimes?

Rip Van Winkle, according to legend, was a ne'er-do-well to begin with. He never worked, drank too much, and lived a shiftless existence, being viewed by townies as something between the town clown and the village idiot. One day, he went up into the hills surrounding his town to actually do something productive with his day—namely, go hunting—when he fell upon a bunch of scurrilous elves who were bowling and boozing. Making sport of him and giving him the greatest lesson of his life, they offered him a nip from their jug of whiskey. Little did he know, as he guzzled the stuff, it was a magical potion that would knock him out. When he woke up, it was twenty years later. Rip had slept his life away.

Sleeping Beauty had only one thing going for her—good looks. She was actually a princess who had been long awaited by her parents, so when she was born, all the fairies came and offered her gifts. One jealous little wretch cursed her, however, and said she would prick her finger on a spindle and die. Luckily, a good fairy was able to soften the death wish and altered it to one hundred years of sleep. Same thing, really. It came to pass that on her fifteenth birthday, the princess did indeed prick her finger and fall into a deep sleep. Luckily, kings' sons were roamers back then, and one of them came and kissed her on the lips, and she awoke. They married, ignoring their one-hundred-year age difference.

First moral of the stories: Don't drink with elves or spin yarn with witches. Second moral: It's better to be awake than asleep.

Help or Hogwash?

SLEEP AIDS

❤ CHAPTER 3 ❤

Nothing works.

It's as simple as that, even if you choose to ignore the overwhelming evidence presented in the previous chapter. Suit yourself. Perhaps you will change your mind after you take a look at the so-called failsafe methods of curing insomnia purported over the decades, which have done nothing more than frustrate the average innocent insomniac at the very least, and, at the very most, waste precious months if not years of creative, productive lives. God knows what amazing feats—nay, miracles—could have been accomplished while whiling away peak hours counting fuzzy sheep.

Dietary Dichotomy

This arena of foolishness, if you take the time to research it, underscores the biggest problem with so-called cures of insomnia—they are rife with contradictions. And if you buy into the conspiracy theory, there is reason for that. Keep us confused enough, and we will second-guess ourselves every time. Or spend thousands of dollars we don't have trying to fix something that isn't fixable. Or perhaps not broken in the first place.

Case in point: One research study suggests a snack before hitting the feathers, adding that the psychological effect of oral satisfaction will relax one directly into slumberland. Hit "advanced search" on your Yahoo search engine to find more ballast for that ship, and lo and behold, another study and several experts caution sternly against eating anything prior to bed, pointing to digestive activity as the last thing needed for a good night's rest. Of course, this begs the larger, existential if not rhetorical and certainly always sarcastic question: "What is a good night's rest, anyway?" (Hint: ask the clown who figured out the chicken-and-the-egg riddle.)

POPULAR FOOD-RELATED CURES FOR NON-SLEEPERS THAT DO NOT WORK INCLUDE:

Drink warm milk.

We'll never know if this works, because the only
people who actually like warm milk are babies.
And they don't sleep through the night, either.

Drink cold milk.

Not recommended for the lactose intolerant.

Drink herbal tea.

And just when you start to fall asleep,
you'll have to jump up to pee.

Drink non-herbal tea.

Is caffeine a sleep aid?

Have a glass of wine or two to relax yourself.

Isn't that called "passing out"?

Smoke yourself to sleep.

Assume cigarettes here, which makes no sense, since nicotine is a stimulant. Or maybe they did mean the illegal stuff.

Avoid caffeine, alcohol, and tobacco.

Are you starting to get it? Which is it?
Drink and smoke, or don't drink and smoke?

It's Your Bed's Fault

You fool. You thought it was you all this time. It's not you. It's your bed, or where it is placed in the room, or the fact that you don't even know how to lie on it, for goodness sake. It's not your overactive, fertile mind working overtime. Can't be that simple. Must be more complicated than that. Before you try any of the tips below, first check under your mattress for a pea. If you can't find one, then drag the blasted bed to the curb.

This rash of insomnia cures points to the biggest affront to insomniacs across the globe—that basically, it's not you at all. You aren't even part of the equation. It's everything else that's responsible. Paint me a victim and call it a day. That's right—not only is there something wrong with you, you poor slob, you can't even do anything about it yourself, short of investing at least a couple of grand into a new bed, a super-duper air ionizer, perhaps an aromatherapy machine that might also play comforting sounds of the playful Orca, an eighteen-foot Jacuzzi to relax your aching muscles and trick them into falling asleep, and a full-time masseuse. Or perhaps it's that damned alarm clock and its glowing face.

SOME POPULAR METHODS THAT ARE PURPORTED TO HELP, MOST LIKELY FROM THE MATTRESS INDUSTRY, INCLUDE:

Sleep in a well-ventilated room
Not really a good idea in winter.

Sleep on a high-quality, firm bed
Adding a layer of bricks on top
of the mattress helps.

Sleep on your back
This works for five-week-old babies.
Try a diaper change, too.
And make sure you have burped.

Take a warm bath

And when you get out all relaxed,
that blast of cold air on wet skin
ought to shock you into sleep.

Get a massage

And then ask the masseuse to sleep over.

Listen to music

Heavy metal or marching music does the trick.

Purify the air in your bedroom

You are clearly low on ions.

Sleep with your head facing north

What were you thinking?

Sleep with your bed pointed south

If combined with the previous tip,
you might sleep with your feet on your pillow.

Avoid illuminated bedroom clocks

Try Braille clocks instead. Easier to read.

Revamping Your Lifestyle

Perhaps even more damaging than believing you are a freak of nature because you can't do anything about your sleeping patterns is thinking that you can. Once you get into the mind-set that you need to change your lifestyle completely to pay abject homage to the hours that you sleep, it's tough to get out of it. Insomniacs can spend years diddling with their schedules, adjusting their lives, and inconveniencing those with whom they share a bed.

Does anyone else see something wrong with this picture? It basically says: alter your waking hours to accommodate your resting ones. Hmm. Isn't that a bit backwards? I mean, what is it you do that is even remotely productive while you're snoring? Shakespeare had it right: "To sleep, perchance to dream." Yes, dreaming. That's the most productive mind activity there is during sleeping. In fact, it's the only productive activity you do while you sleep. Unless you astral project.

Basically, the assumption is you are doing something wrong while you are awake that is leading to why you can't sleep. So, figure out what it is that you are doing wrong, and fix it.

SOME SUGGESTIONS FROM DOCTOR "I-AM-SO-AN-EXPERT-AND-I-HAVE-A-PH. D.-TO-PROVE-IT, SO-THERE" INCLUDE:

Get physical exercise during the day

Doesn't everyone? Unless you're holed up in
a hospital bed, it's tough not to get at least
some physical exercise.

Keep regular bedtime hours

Again with the judgment. What if your regular bedtime hours
are 11:00 pm to 1:00 am, and 4:00 am to 6:00 am?
It could be argued that those *are* your regular hours.

Don't sleep in

This makes no sense. You would think they would
want you to, if you fall asleep at 4:30 a.m.

Get up earlier in the morning
Is 1:00 a.m. early enough?

Avoid naps
Especially while driving, operating heavy machinery,
or while pregnant. Good luck on the last one.

Don't watch television
or read before you go to bed
Better to just lie there in the dark, worrying,
than educate or entertain yourself.
Heck, they don't even want you to have a good time.

Establish a bedtime ritual
Consider re-enacting a Hopi sleep dance
or offering a young virgin to the gods of Somnia.

Utterly Useless Wastes of Time

Once in bed, the experts have even concocted a whole slew of things you can do to not only waste your time, but that will ultimately result in one thing: keeping you awake. Let's add: keeping you awake doing mind-numbing, moronic things. And if you believe in the conspiracy theory (and by now, you should), keeping you awake doing mind-numbing, moronic things rather than saving the world—is that what you want?

The bed is only for sleeping
If that's true, then where, pray tell,
should you do all of the following things?
In the outhouse? Outside on the front lawn?

Toe wiggling
This makes absolutely no sense,
unless you have been rendered paralyzed.
Then this might be considered a miracle.

Rub your stomach

And when you realize how fat you've gotten,
you'll have something else to worry about
while you can't sleep.

Progressive relaxation

Balderdash. This is physically impossible to accomplish
and will just lead you to obsessing about what is wrong with
you, since you can't completely relax the crown of your head.

Deep breathing exercises

You run the risk of hyperventilation, but this does work
if you consider passing out falling asleep.

Visualize something peaceful

And then get angry beyond belief when you can't.

Visualize something boring

As if lying there awake with nothing to do isn't dull enough.

Imagine it's time to get up

Why?

Write your thoughts out on paper

While this is meant to rid those thoughts from your mind,
the opposite happens. You start obsessing about all of them.

Yawn

Not a bad idea, if you don't mind getting hiccups.

Have sex, alone or with others

Pardon me? Isn't the bed only for sleeping, kemosabe?

Count backwards

Once you get to zero for the tenth time,
you will realize just how effective this method is.

Use earplugs

Unless your house is located three feet from
an active train track or all-night shooting range,
earplugs are very annoying.

Don't think

Well, Einstein, if we knew how to do this,
we wouldn't be lying awake all night.

CHAPTER 4

Stop feeling like you are flawed.

Lose the victim cloak, for goodness sake, would you? It is highly unattractive, and while sleep freaks would love to keep you sublimated, it gets old for the rest of us empowered insomniacs. As the old Christian saying goes, "Get off the wood, someone else needs the cross."

You are not a victim. You are one of the heaven-sent few who can actually function on little sleep. You have been given what others have longed for—more hours in the day. Do something with them.

Getting With the Program

Undoubtedly the best way to tackle your insomnia is the "If you can't beat 'em, join 'em" theory that most veteran insomniacs eventually come to embrace. But caution here: weaning yourself off trying to get sleep is a process. And it requires discipline and the use of positive affirmations. There is a belief in insomniac circles that while those who can get by on little sleep are a superior breed, they are also a fickle lot. Many are super-sensitive, prone to emotional outbursts and crying jags, bursts of temper, bizarre episodes of sudden, unexplainable bouts of exhaustion, visions and hallucinations, and the desire to close one's eyes while driving.

IF YOU EXPERIENCE ANY OF THESE, PLEASE TAKE A NAP. (OR GET A GOOD NIGHT'S SLEEP, FOR CRIMINY'S SAKE.)

1. Be gentle with yourself.

It may take a while to discard the myths and just embrace the essence of your gift. Give yourself time. And remember, we are just differently oriented.

2. Relax and accept.

If you have to lie in bed, don't fight the inevitable; use your time wisely. There are plenty of things you can do while lying in bed—and they don't have to be mind-numbing exercises in stupidity. Be productive, for goodness sake, even if you are lying on your latest purchase, your new Craftmatic adjustable bed. Forget the sheep. Try one of the following:

3. Learn a new language.

Try counting backward from one million—in Latin. This will require you to learn Latin, of course, which is a win-win any way you look at it—especially if you want to retire someday and study scripture in its native language. Or teach the root words of much of the vocabulary in the romance languages. And by the time you reach 'unus,' or one, it will be 6:00 a.m. anyway and time to get up.

4. Pray or meditate.

Do you have any idea how many souls you can save in an hour or two of heavy-duty praying during the time of night that only you and a handful of cloistered nuns and silent monks are doing vigil? It doesn't matter what faith you are or how you pray—well, save those who sacrifice animals for this endeavor. Just for hoots and hollers, pick some jerk you really hate, and send a few loving zappers his or her way. You might even be able to get in several novenas if you're really awake. Who knows? Heck, after a few months, you could even accomplish world peace, end all wars, and stave off pestilence. Hey, stranger things have happened.

5. Reconnect with your childhood.

This is always a fun pastime. While you are lying in bed, try to remember all the horrible things that your parents inflicted upon you as a child. Or if you unfortunately come from a functional family, think of the miserable kids from your neighborhood who called you "pickle nose" or your first date who dumped you and then turned around and dated your best friend. Get really fired up while lying in bed, and then blame all of them for your inability to sleep. At that point, you can have the epiphany that they truly have helped you because now you don't have to fritter your life away snoozing—you can be somebody. Channel that energy into something positive—like making a million dollars, just to show 'em.

6. Reach out and touch someone.

Install a phone extension near your bed. Or keep the cell phone charged and within reaching distance from your pillow. You can do a lot of damage by calling folks in the wee hours of the morning—especially those from the previous tip. If you're serious about actually chatting it up, try dialing another time zone where someone might actually be awake. If you're into pranking, then call your next-door neighbor and tell him you just saw his wife crawling back into the bedroom window. We're talking truckloads of fun.

Making the Time Work for You!

If none of these work, then there are countless things you can do to not only improve the world but also yourself. Just remember, the hours between dusk and dawn aren't only for drinking shots of Mad Dog, playing Parcheesi, wiggling your toes, watching infomercials, and thinking obsessive thoughts. They can be productive, too. So when your eyes pop open at 2:00 a.m. or if you have tossed and turned for an hour and can't find a comfortable position, get up! Get out of bed. Forget obsessing about how you can sabotage your boss. Stop counting in between your spouse's snores. Don't watch one more infomercial about how you can make gazillions by spending only one dollar on real estate. Use these hours wisely. These can be, and oftentimes are, your most creative hours. Don't waste them on furthering your neurosis.

Wake time is work time. Why be so submissive, working inside the parameters that time zones and narrow-minded corporations have built for you? Two to four extra hours in the wee hours of the day can pile up to an average of two extra work days a week. Two whole extra days. Think of all the work you can accomplish, regardless of what it is you do for a living. You have a computer: get to work. Why wait for the morning? You might surprise yourself. You're firing on all cylinders now. Take advantage of it.

1. Expand your career horizons.

Ever consider doing work in Papua, New Guinea? Of course not, because you spent the last few years feeling sorry for yourself because you can't sleep. Oh, boo-hoo. Untie yourself from the train tracks, Nell, and start making hay while the sun ain't shining. There are multiple work opportunities out there for you, and you don't even have to quit your day job. It's daylight somewhere in this world.

Now, you just have to figure out where. It's kind of like the popular drawings *Where's Waldo?* Cast your line and find new business in a distant, exotic land. Depending on your line of work, you could be looking at increasing your revenue by a significant margin.

2. Make a new pal.

Don't feel like working? Okay. Maybe you'd cotton more to an instant messaging pen pal or striking up an e-mail friendship with someone living where it technically is yesterday. Your new friend in Thimpu, Bhutan, will think you're a mindreader, wowing him about the events that occurred while he was asleep. There are thousands of people online in need of a friend. Granted, most of them are probably unsavory, depraved predators and wannabe mass murderers. But this begs the larger question: how long do you want to live a sheltered life? Reach out and befriend the friendless stalker.

3. Pick up a hobby.

Insomniacs never have to worry about not having enough time to master a new skill or adopt a new hobby. With all those extra hours normally wasted snoring, you can finally learn how to macramé. Online courses abound, as well as do-it-yourself kits. Don't limit yourself to the small stuff. The Internet has opened a whole new world to learning. Tired of being a mechanic? Try the online "Brain Surgery for Dummies" course. Six weeks and you could be lasering tumors. You don't have to make a career of it, for goodness sake, but think of the extra coin you could earn on the side! Internet not your thing?

There are plenty of open-all-night venues right in your home town that might tickle your fancy. Plenty of insomniacs have learned the fine art of pole and lap dancing in those hours that their loved ones are snoozing. The world is truly your oyster.

4. Spend time with your family.

Who doesn't whine that they need more quality time with the kids? What spouse doesn't like to feel special? So what if it's 3:30 in the morning. Rouse those brats, tell them you love them and then read 'em a bedtime story to try to get them back to sleep. Or take them out for a wee morning snack. Some fast food joints are open all night. Or jostle the spouse awake and spend some quality time discussing home remortgaging options, world politics, whether or not you still love each other, and the new joys of sharing something like insomnia together. Get to know each other better than you ever thought possible.

5. Launch a home improvement project.

No time to work on re-shingling the roof during the daylight hours, and weekends are just too short? There's plenty of time late at night and in the wee hours of the morning. The gutters could always use a cleaning; the house, a new coat of paint; the car, a fine soapy wash; the lawn, a solid mowing. Don't buy into the belief that you need daylight to do large-scale inside or outside projects. That's simply not true. Hook up some outdoor lighting, fire up the mower, and get that lawn done. Worried about what your neighbors might think? Why? They don't care what you think. And at the very least, they'll just think of you as being charmingly eccentric.

6. Start your own Wide-Awake Club.

Support groups are one way to change the stigma surrounding a misunderstood condition and empower the stigmatized. Finding insomniacs in cyberspace isn't that hard. Now you just have to organize them into a loosely knit group of night owlers. Make your own rules, set up your specific charter. Collaborate your efforts so that if you are tired of spending those wakeful, late-night hours alone, you can find safety and power in numbers. There is no limit to what you can accomplish or to what you can do.

7. Wish upon a star.

Hey, you're up—why not learn about the night sky? Unless you're in Alaska during the time of year when the sun never sets, you should have ample constellations upon which to gaze during the wee hours of the morning. Can you find Orion? Ursa Major? How about Monocerus? If you get frustrated, just pick out one or two bright spots and sing "Twinkle, twinkle, little star." This is how Galileo got started.

Are You an Insomniac?

In case you aren't already well aware that you are, here's a pop quiz to get you out of denial and into "non-sleepers rule" mode:

1. Have you ever purchased a cubic zirconium pendant set in a real 14-carat gold-plated setting on QVC at 2:00 a.m. because it was the most gorgeous thing you'd ever seen and you just had to have it?
A. Yes
B. No
C. No, but I have purchased a complete home gym. Does that count?

2. When lying awake in the wee hours of the morning, have you ever counted more than 624,000 sheep?
A. Yes
B. No
C. I think so, but I lost count.

3. Have you tried every prescriptive sleeping drug on the market and are still desperately seeking the "one that really works"?

A. Yes
B. No
C. Not until just now

4. Do you wonder if you are addicted to sleeping aids?
A. Yes
B. No
C. Just what do you mean by addicted?

5. On average, how many hours do you sleep a night?
A. 2-4
B. 6-8
C. 16 minutes

6. Do you need alcohol to help you fall asleep?
A. Yes
B. No
C. No, thank you. I have sleeping pills.

Answer key: *If you answered A or C to any of these questions, congratulations and welcome. You are the person this book was written for. If you answered B, you're way too normal for the rest of us. What, are you feeling sorry for an insomniac in your life? Buy them this book so they can feel empowered.*

Animal Facts

Did you know that cows can
sleep while standing up, but they
only dream when lying down?

Whales and dolphins are
conscious breathers,
and they need to keep
breathing while they sleep,
so only half of their brains
sleep at a time.

Sharks never sleep. Well,
not like we humans do.
They have restful periods but
do continuously swim during
that time, so what's your excuse?

Epilogue

The goal behind this book has been to look at what heretofore has caused great angst and suffering among non-sleepers. It has been to take insomnia out of the box that it has been so handily stuffed into, flip it around a few times, and reconsider it. For at some point, chronic insomniacs all reach the "I'm mad as hell and I can't take it any more" stage. It is at that very juncture that this book steps in. Rather than beating the tar out of ourselves, maybe, just maybe, we have been given a gift. A gift that other mortals pine for and yet is ever elusive—the gift of more hours in the day. A new day is dawning, but it doesn't have to be when the sun comes up. As insomniacs rise up and embrace the new definition of our former malady, we walk in the light of empowerment and enlightenment. We don't have to suffer anymore. We should embrace change and our inability to sleep and do something with that time rather than mindlessly counting sheep.

After all, this might be it. As Leonard Cohen, Canadian poet and songwriter has said, "The last refuge of the insomniac is a sense of superiority to the sleeping world." Go forth and be superior. But be careful not to wake up the others.

Hopefully, this book has helped to quell some fears of fellow non-sleepers, bolstered self-esteem, and opened the door to limitless potential, which will allow insomniacs to become masters of the universe. Or at least of the nights.

About
the Author

Lenore Skomal is a career insomniac. In other words, her insomnia has substantially fueled her career. As a young child, most of her homework was finished between the hours of 2 and 4 o'clock in the morning. She learned early on that her curse was really her blessing, and she wishes to share her epiphany with the sleepless world. An award-winning author, columnist, and career journalist of twenty-five years, she has published nine books so far—five with Cider Mill Press. She also teaches writing at two universities and conducts public seminars on writing. If she slept the requisite seven hours a night, how would she be able to do all of this?

About
Cider Mill Press

Good ideas ripen with time. From seed to harvest, Cider Mill Press strives to bring fine reading, information, and entertainment together between the covers of its creatively crafted books. Our Cider Mill bears fruit twice a year, publishing a new crop of titles each spring and fall.

CIDER MILL PRESS

BOOK PUBLISHERS

Where good books
are ready for press

Visit us on the web at:
www.cidermillpress.com

or write to us at:
12 Port Farm Road
Kennebunkport, Maine 04046